DID YOU KNOW?

by Barbara Seuling

Xerox Education Publications
Middletown, Connecticut

Acknowledgments

The author gratefully acknowledges the following among the many sources of material for this book.

P. 10, #4; p. 15, #2; p. 22, #1; p. 40, #2; p. 44, #1; p. 47, #3: abridged and adapted from *The Story of Language* by Mario Pei. Copyright © 1965, 1949 by Mario Pei. Reprinted by permission of J. B. Lippincott Company.

P. 5, #3; p. 11, #2; p. 14, #3; p. 25, #2; p. 27, #3; p. 28, #1; p. 29, #4; p. 45, #2; p. 46, #3; p. 56, #1; p. 61, #1; p. 63, #2: used with permission of the *National Enquirer.*

P. 31, #3; p. 45, #3; p. 57, #4: *Smithsonian* magazine, reprinted by permission.

P. 12, #2; p. 21, #4; p. 32, #1; p. 35, #3; p. 38, #2; p. 40, #1; p. 66, #4; p. 71, #5; p. 76, #3: "The Hollywood Squares," Heatter-Quigley, Inc. Used with permission.

P. 36, #5; p. 67, #6; p. 75, #1: from *National Geographic,* by permission of the National Geographic Society.

By permission of *Natural History* magazine: P. 45, #1, April, 1976, *Journey of a Seventeenth-Century Cannon* by Christopher L. Hallowell, p. 76. P. 48, #1, April, 1976, *Ladders, Bushes, and Human Evolution* by Stephen Jay Gould, p. 24. P. 51, #3, April, 1976, *The "Fever-Bark" Tree* by Richard M. Klein, p. 10. P. 71, #3, August-September 1974, *How Old Is the Universe?* by Robert Jastrow, p. 80.

P. 7, #5; p. 10, #3; p. 13, #2: *American Farm & Home Almanac.* Reprinted with permission.

P. 10, #2; p. 19, #1, #2; p. 20, #3, #4; p. 30, #6; p. 34, #5; p. 35, #6; p. 44, #3; p. 47, #5; p. 59, #4; p. 62, #3: *The Columbia Encyclopedia,* Columbia University Press. Reprinted with permission.

P. 37, #2; p. 48, #3: *Evolution of the Alphabet from A to Z,* Westvaco Corporation. Used with permission.

P. 6, #4; p. 11, #1; p. 14, #5; p. 20, #2; p. 28, #5; p. 42, #2; p. 46, #2: *The First Book of Surprising Facts* by Frances N. Chrystie, Franklin Watts, Inc. Reprinted with permission.

P. 41, #1; p. 76, #4: *Popular Mechanics,* July 1976. Used with permission.

P. 23, #1; p. 32, #2; p. 74, #5; p. 75, #4: *The Old Farmer's Almanac,* published by Yankee, Inc., Dublin, N. H. Used with permission.

P. 78, #1: *The People's Almanac* by Irving Wallace and David Wallechinsky, © 1975 Doubleday & Company. Reprinted with permission.

P. 23, #2: Chamber of Commerce, Vineland, N. J.

P. 55, #3: "A Greeting from Coney Island," by Richard F. Snow, © 1975 American Heritage Publishing Co., Inc. Reprinted by permission from *American Heritage* (September 1975).

Acknowledgments *(cont.)*

P. 44, #5: Scholastic Magazines, Inc. Used by permission.

P. 7, #2; p. 35, #2; p. 62, #4: from *Facts and Fictions About Coins* by Leon Lindheim, © 1967, World Publishing Company. Reprinted by permission of Thomas Y. Crowell Company, Inc.

P. 15, #1; p. 43, #1; p. 53, #3: from Ripley's *Believe It or Not!* Used with permission of Ripley International Limited, Toronto.

P. 6, #2; p. 32, #5; p. 78, #2, #3: *Encyclopedia of World Travel,* © 1961, 1967, Doubleday & Company. Reprinted with permission.

P. 8, #2; p. 16, #5; p. 51, #5; p. 78, #3: © 1965 American Heritage Publishing Co., Inc. Reprinted by permission from *The New Pictorial Encyclopedic Guide to the United States.*

P. 77, #2, #3, #4; p. 78, #4: *Grab-A-Pencil,* © 1958, 1971, Hart Publishing Co.

P. 77, #5; p. 78, #5: *The North American Almanac,* North American Almanac Co., Chicago.

There are about 3,000 languages spoken in the world.

Some people believe that a name with seven letters in it is lucky.

In 1974, the United States Postal Service handled 90.1 billion pieces of mail.

The deepest body of water is the Pacific Ocean, and the deepest part of that is along the Marianas Trench near the Philippine Islands, where it is approximately 36,000 feet deep.

Hawaii is the only state in the Union where coffee is grown commercially.

The estimated age of the earth is somewhere between 3 and 5 billion years.

Pirates wore earrings because they believed that earrings improved their vision.

The world's only living sextuplets are Jason, David, Emma, Grant, Nicolette, and Elizabeth Rosenkowitz, born on January 11, 1974.

The ancient Romans used safety pins.

For three years, 1875 to 1878, there was a 20-cent United States coin.

A university study shows that 72 percent of Americans are happy.

President Ford, Rembrandt, Helen Keller, Freddie Prinze, and Phyllis Diller were all born under the sign of Cancer (June 21 to July 22).

Jumbo, a giant elephant brought to America by P. T. Barnum in the days when few Americans had seen a live elephant, was killed when a freight train ran into her. Her skeleton was put on display in the American Museum of Natural History in New York City.

The surface temperature of the sun is about 11,000° F.

Until 1819 the Hawaiian language had never been written.

The platypus has a bill like a duck and webbed feet like a duck, but it is actually a mammal.

The name *Blumenthal* means "Blossom Valley."

As far back as biblical times, almonds were used as gifts.

When some species of flies mate, the male brings the female tiny food parcels to keep her busy unwrapping and eating, to keep her from eating him.

The giraffe is the tallest animal in the world.

Some people believe that big feet are a sign of intelligence.

When the volcano Mount Pelée erupted on the island of Martinique in 1902, every inhabitant of the town of St. Pierre was killed except for two men, one of whom was in a prison cell with stone walls so thick that the heat and shock did not kill him.

In 1752 there was an 11-day difference between the calendars used by England and those used by the rest of the European continent.

Betsy Ross and Paul Revere were born on the same day of the year: New Year's Day, January 1.

The Aztec Indian language is still spoken today in some parts of Mexico.

A system of musical notation was invented for transcribing the songs of birds.

Mount Everest in the Himalayas is the highest mountain on land, at 29,000 feet; but the highest mountain on earth is Mauna Kea, in the Pacific Ocean. Only about 14,000 feet of it are visible, but from its base on the ocean floor it rises 45,000 feet.

Certain people in the Caucasus of the U.S.S.R., or the Soviet Union, live well past the age of 100.

It is illegal in Massachusetts to use tomatoes in clam chowder.

If a starfish loses an arm, it can grow another one.

Former President Dwight D. Eisenhower, former First Lady Eleanor Roosevelt, Mickey Mantle, Helen Reddy, and John Lennon were born under the sign of Libra (September 23 to October 22).

Singer John Denver was born on New Year's Eve.

A baby sponge has tiny hairs on it to help it swim.

More people live on the tiny islands of Hawaii (6,450 square miles) than in Alaska, the largest state in the Union, which is 586,412 square miles.

A man who started a vacuum-cleaner empire and a President of the United States had the same name: Herbert Hoover.

On Santa Cruz Island in the South Pacific, feathers are used as money.

Scientists believe that the seven continents were once connected and split into pieces as the surface of the earth moved. If you look at a map or a globe, you can see that many land areas will almost fit together like the pieces of a puzzle.

The first color movie in 3-D was *The House of Wax,* with Vincent Price.

The voice of baby Pebbles in TV's cartoon series *The Flintstones* is that of actress Sally Struthers, who later became well-known as Gloria on *All in the Family.*

In 1975, 25 million electronic calculators were sold in the United States.

Crickets have no ears.

The King of Siam had 370 children at the time of his death in 1910.

In this country, a *C* on a water faucet means *cold,* but in France it stands for *chaud,* in Spain it stands for *caliente,* and in Italy it stands for *caldo,* all of which mean HOT.

The Turks of ancient Anatolia fed the cooked tongues of birds to children who were slow in learning to talk.

St. Augustine, Florida, settled in 1565, is the oldest city in America.

George Washington, Marian Anderson, Alexander Graham Bell, Bobby Fischer, and Elizabeth Taylor were born under the sign of Pisces (February 19 to March 20).

The first English language dictionary was compiled by Dr. Samuel Johnson and published in 1755.

There are thousands of coyotes within the city limits of Los Angeles.

When you are at the South Pole, all directions are north.

The horns of the rhinoceros are really hard masses of hair, not bone.

The Seminole Indians of Florida are technically still at war with the United States.

It is about 238,900 miles to the moon.

In 1876, a train ride from New York to San Francisco took more than 83 hours.

Sir Winston Churchill, the great English statesman, was a terrible failure in school and liked playing with his toy soldiers more than studying. Later, he became one of the world's finest leaders.

At the time of the American Revolution, about one-fifth of the people in the Colonies were black.

The first income tax imposed by the Federal Government in 1861 was declared unconstitutional and was removed.

The most frequently consulted catalog cards in the central branch of the New York Public Library are *astrology, drugs, witchcraft,* and *Shakespeare.*

Mozart and Beethoven wrote musical works for the harmonica.

When the fork was introduced into England, many people laughed at it and thought it ridiculous.

The lowest point in the United States is in Death Valley, California, where it is 280 feet below sea level.

Old German playing cards used the symbols heart, leaf, bell, and acorn, instead of heart, club, diamond, and spade.

Doris Day, Thomas Jefferson, Hans Christian Andersen, Elton John, and Betty Ford were born under the sign of Aries, the Ram (March 21 to April 19).

Dancer Fred Astaire sometimes repeated a dance scene 35 times before he was satisfied that it was good enough for the film he was making.

The full and original name of the city of Los Angeles in California was *El Pueblo de Nuestra Señora la Reina de los Angeles de Porciuncola.*

Coca leaves, chewed by the Incas in ancient times, contain a small amount of the narcotic cocaine. When the Spanish conquered the Incas, only the nobility were permitted to chew the leaves.

Each new pope is given a special "fisherman's ring," which is destroyed when he dies.

The lovely Christmas rose that blossoms only at Christmastime contains a deadly poison.

Eskimos once used shark teeth for barber tools.

Peter Stuyvesant, early governor of New York, lost his leg in a battle on the Caribbean Island of Saint Maarten. It is known now that the leg is buried on the island of Curaçao, also in the Caribbean.

Africa's 4,000-mile-long Nile River is the longest in the world.

The love bird is actually antisocial.

The first United States flag was raised by George Washington at Cambridge, Massachusetts, on January 2, 1776. It had 13 stripes, red and white, and a blue canton bearing the crosses of Saint George and Saint Andrew.

Chinese custom prohibits a son from using the second character of his father's name in writing.

In the 19th century, when bodies were needed by doctors for medical study, suppliers were paid a flat fee for an adult's corpse and were paid by the inch for a child's body.

The woman who invented Mother's Day, Anna M. Jarvis, grew to be very sorry she had created the holiday because so many people were interested in making money out of it.

The town of Vineland, New Jersey, holds an annual dandelion festival.

Philosopher Jeremy Bentham ordered in his will that after he died his body be used for medical study, and when that was done, that the skeleton be reassembled on wires for anatomy lessons. Also in his will was a requirement that his head be mummified and stuck on top of the skeleton and the whole thing presented at each meeting of Bentham's organization. His wishes were carried out.

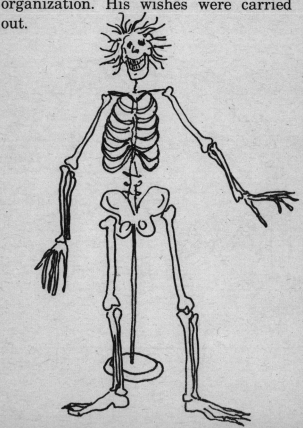

Theodore Roosevelt, Marie Antoinette, Pablo Picasso, Madame Curie, and Charles Bronson were born under the sign of Scorpio (Oct. 23 to Nov. 21).

Americans buy more mouthwash than any other people.

The ancient Mayans of Mexico wrote and illustrated books.

The author of *Frankenstein* was a 19-year-old woman named Mary Shelley.

Legendary film star Greta Garbo once had a job lathering faces in a barber shop in Sweden.

Cape Cod was named after Captain Bartholomew Gosnold's remark in 1602 that on making harbor there, he was "battered with cod."

It takes 300 gallons of water to make one barrel of beer.

Astronaut Neil Armstrong was the first human being to walk on the moon.

In the year 1977 Mickey Mouse celebrates his 50th birthday.

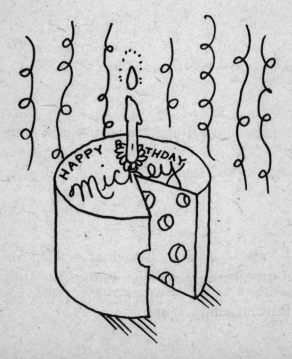

On November 28, 1796, Thomas Jefferson's ink froze.

One of the earliest known pieces of art is the *Venus of Willendorf,* a sculpture of a woman, dating back at least to 10,000 B.C. and possibly to as early as 35,000 B.C.

According to the Department of Defense, 4,435 people died in battle in the Revolutionary War.

Hamburgers started in New Haven, Connecticut, at the turn of the century, when the proprietor of a diner invented them to use up leftovers.

The ruler of the British Commonwealth has two birthdays, one on the actual date of birth and the other on an official date in June.

If a measuring rod were stuck through the center of the earth, it would measure just about 7,900 miles from pole to pole.

Queen Victoria, John F. Kennedy, Richard Thomas, Martha Washington, and Bob Dylan were born under the sign of Gemini (May 21-June 20).

The human arm contains 32 bones.

The Queen Emma Bridge on the island of Curacao is on pontoons and swings open about 30 times a day. People are known to have become seasick walking across this bridge.

The Mayans had a calendar in ancient times more accurate than the one we use today, with 18 months of 20 days each and 5 days left over for evening out the year. The extra days were used for festivals, or holidays.

The koala is native only to Australia because it eats only eucalyptus leaves, and the eucalyptus tree is native only to Australia.

There is some evidence that the brothers Cosmas and Damian in the third century performed a leg transplant.

Alaska, the largest state in the Union, is more than double the size of the next largest state, Texas, yet has the smallest population of the 50 states.

Between 1935 and 1971 the United States did not mint any silver dollars.

Jacqueline Onassis' birthstone is a ruby.

One out of every two persons in the United States owns a car.

Abraham Lincoln, Babe Ruth, Susan B. Anthony, Thomas Edison, and Bill Russell were born under the sign of Aquarius (January 20-February 18).

Wigs became popular in France during the reign of Louis XIII because he was bald and wore wigs.

There is some evidence that the cavemen made music.

Benjamin Franklin said, in *Poor Richard's Almanack,* "To lengthen thy life, lessen thy meals."

Scientists have proved that children can make enough noise to harm a listener's health.

The United States Post Office once lost the body of a man shipped to a cemetery. It was forced to pay the man's family a fine of $15.

If a dollar bill is torn, it can be redeemed for its full face value if the remaining piece contains at least 3/5 of the original.

Owls eat mice whole, but spit up the teeth, claws, bones, and fur.

In the shop of the Bronx Zoo in New York City you can buy paintings done by the chimpanzees for $5 apiece.

Miami Beach, Florida, has no cemeteries.

At one time Walt Disney was the voice for all of his cartoon characters.

The first space passenger was a dog, Laika, who orbited the earth in the Soviet Union's Sputnik II.

Charlie Chaplin is known in France as "Charlot."

In England in the 1600's, to discourage people from clipping the edges off valuable coins, a rim was put around the coins stamped THE PENALTY FOR CLIPPING THIS COIN IS DEATH.

Magician John Scarne is so expert at card tricks that the police have called on him to help expose dishonest players and gambling houses.

Valerie Harper's birthstone is a sardonyx.

A one-cent postage stamp issued in 1856 by British Guiana is now one of the world's rarest stamps, valued at about $325,000.

In 800 B.C. during a revolution, the Persians used a flag made from a blacksmith's apron.

When a heavy fog lifted in London in 1962, after four days, 106 deaths were related directly to it.

The ancient Carthaginians used money made of leather.

John Wayne once won a Shakespeare contest in southern California.

Some shark meat is toxic, and when fed to sled dogs can make them "drunk."

Ink originated more than 4,000 years ago.

Ball-bearing skate wheels were invented in the 1880's.

The great Cherokee Indian chief Sequoyah invented the first written language for the Cherokee, consisting of an 85-character alphabet.

The pony express lasted only 18 months.

The richest silver mine in Nevada was discovered in 1859 by a sheepherder, Henry Comstock, who was nicknamed "Old Pancake."

Winston Churchill, Sammy Davis, Jr., Joe DiMaggio, Louisa May Alcott, and Rich Little were born under the sign of Sagittarius (November 22-December 21).

The tongue of a full-grown blue whale weighs about the same as the combined weight of 40 full-grown men.

The royal water lily, found in the Amazon River, has a pad that can grow to more than 6 feet wide and is strong enough to support the weight of a small person.

The Phoenicians named the letter *C* in their alphabet after the camel (*gimel*) and gave it a symbol that represented the camel's long neck.

The weight of the planet earth is estimated at around 6,000,000,000,000,-000,000,000 tons.

Miami Beach, Florida, which is only about 7 square miles in size, has nearly 400 hotels that can accommodate 150,000 guests each night.

For reasons unexplained, people who are born in February tend to live longer than anyone else.

The United States Government runs a marijuana plantation in Mississippi ... the only legal one in the country.

Leonardo da Vinci, master painter of the 15th century, dissected about 30 corpses in secret and made drawings of everything he saw for the purpose of studying anatomy. At the time, even medical students had trouble learning about the human body because dissecting corpses was not permitted.

Wyoming's nickname is the "Equality State," because it was the first state to allow women to vote.

The kiwi, a bird found only in New Zealand, has no wings and therefore cannot fly.

At night the temperature on the moon drops to about 200° below zero.

Alexander Hamilton, first U.S. Secretary of the Treasury, was named Alexander Levine when he was born, but changed his name to that of his stepfather.

Chiefs on certain South Sea islands have the unique power of reserving certain words in the language for their own personal use.

At the Centennial festivities in Philadelphia in 1876, a new drink was demonstrated, made from a recipe calling for roots, plants, and berries. The man promoting the new product was pharmacist Charles Hires, and the drink became popular as root beer.

Chicken farmers who tried to save money on plucking by breeding featherless chickens ended up spending more money feeding them. The poor chickens ran around so much trying to keep warm that they worked up a bigger appetite and had to eat more.

Cicely Tyson's birthstone is a turquoise.

The intestines of a full-grown human being are about 25 to 30 feet long.

The planet Uranus, discovered in 1781 by Frederick William Herschel, circles the sun approximately once every 80 years.

The Statue of Liberty's mouth is 3 feet wide.

Movies are actually an illusion. A series of still pictures is projected on a screen in such rapid succession that the human eye perceives them as showing continuous motion.

Napoleon Bonaparte, Amelia Earhart, Alfred Hitchcock, and Jacqueline Onassis were born under the sign of Leo (July 23 to August 22).

The word *hurry* was invented by William Shakespeare.

In some parts of the American Colonies, celebrating Christmas was against the law.

On some South Sea islands it is taboo to mention the names of the dead.

Martin Luther King, Joan of Arc, John Denver, Clara Barton, and Muhammad Ali were born under the sign of Capricorn (December 22 to January 19).

Originally, some of the Pilgrims set sail in the *Speedwell,* but it was unseaworthy and had to return to port. The passengers were crowded onto the already packed *Mayflower,* and she set sail alone.

Harvard was the first college in the U.S., established in 1636.

In a poll taken among high school students, more than 60 percent thought that the TV family viewing period was a good idea.

When the New York World Trade Center was being built, artifacts found in the cellar excavation included teacups, smoking pipes, and ship's timbers.

A doctor in Pakistan developed a transplant operation that enables blind people to see through the corneas of fish.

A farmer in North Carolina grew a 197-pound watermelon.

There is a law in Arizona that protects Gila monsters.

The closest of all relatives are siblings — brothers and sisters.

Statistics show that Americans bought more than 3 billion pounds of candy in 1974.

Some people feel that squeaky shoes are a sign that the shoes have not been paid for.

The drinking toast originated in England with the serving of Christmas punch in a huge bowl that had pieces of toast floating on top.

There are 33 major languages spoken in India.

Elephants have eyelashes that are about 3 inches long.

Webster's Dictionary was published originally for those who had mastered *Noah Webster's Spelling Book.*

The oldest human fossils, found in Tanzania, indicate that the human race is about 3½ million years old.

The Caspian Sea in the U.S.S.R. is actually a lake.

The letter *A* was named *alef,* or *ox,* by the Phoenicians and given a symbol representing ox horns.

A 130-year-old former slave, who was still living in Florida in 1972, remembered a job he had had picking fruit when he was only 113.

President Franklin Delano Roosevelt's birthstone was the garnet.

The great Greek philosopher Socrates was condemned to death for corrupting the morals of the youth of Athens, but because he was such a respected citizen, he was offered the special privilege of suicide so that he could die with dignity.

One hundred percent of Greenland's population is literate.

Tobacco, discovered in Santo Domingo in 1496, was introduced into England in 1583.

Japan, smaller in area than the state of Montana, has more than 130 times as many people.

There are more television sets used in the United States than telephones, refrigerators, or bathtubs.

Henry VIII had a special penalty for kitchen help caught in plots to harm their masters: He boiled them in a huge cauldron.

Most men part their hair on the left side.

Millionaire Howard Hughes was born on Christmas Eve, December 24.

A natural bridge of shoals, called Adam's Bridge, connects India and Ceylon.

More soldiers were downed by malaria than by bullets in the Spanish-American War in 1898.

The stork is a sign of good luck to Europeans, and many people have constructed stork nests on their rooftops to invite them to nest there.

Hawaii is sometimes called "Orchid Island" because of the 22,000 varieties of orchids grown there.

Henry Kissinger's birthstone is an emerald.

Dolphins are not fish; they are mammals.

If you weigh 50 pounds on Earth, you would weigh 132 pounds on the planet of Jupiter.

The oldest literature on earth is believed to be the *Epic of Gilgamesh*, which is dated back to the Sumerians of ancient Mesopotamia.

For Easter each year, Nicholas, the last czar of Russia, gave his wife, Alexandra, a specially designed Easter egg, fashioned by the renowned jeweler Faberge. The egg was decorated with gold and precious jewels.

It was once a custom among German royalty to raise another boy along with a royal prince who would serve as a substitute and be spanked when the real prince misbehaved.

A bald eagle's nest has been found that measured 9½ feet in diameter and was 20 feet deep.

Queen Elizabeth I, Jesse James, Greta Garbo, Jimmy Connors, and Robert Blake were born under the sign of Virgo (August 23 to September 22).

The postcard was first introduced in 1873.

The scales of herring are used in the manufacture of some nail polish.

George Melies, the 19th-century Frenchman who is called the "father of the movies," invented much of the trick camera work that was used in later films such as the original *King Kong*.

Budapest, the capital of Hungary, was originally two cities, Buda and Pest.

The first roller coaster was built on Coney Island in Brooklyn in 1884.

There is snow on the equator.

The smallest penguins in the world are the fairy penguins of Phillip Island off the southern coast of Australia.

The electric chair was invented by a man who wanted to be humane to condemned prisoners and save them from hanging.

The "Star-Spangled Banner" was written by author Francis Scott Key on the back of an envelope.

Greenland is the world's largest island, with 840,000 square miles. It is owned by Denmark, which is about 1/50 Greenland's size.

In 1970, about 1,800 gallons of water were used each day for each person in the U.S.A.

Queen Elizabeth II, William Shakespeare, Willie Mays, Cloris Leachman, and Stevie Wonder were born under the sign of Taurus (April 20 to May 20).

England produced the world's first stick-on postage stamps in 1840.

Socrates, the great Greek philosopher, could not read or write.

In the second century B.C. Hipparchus catalogued more than a thousand stars.

Noted film fiend Vincent Price confesses to having met his wife in a cemetery.

The first circus was a place where the entertainment might consist of watching slaves being torn to pieces by vicious animals.

Some people say that if your shoe-laces are untied, someone is thinking of you.

Benjamin Franklin, perhaps the most well-known of all the American patriots in Colonial times, had a son, William, who was a leader of the Tories (those on the side of the British Crown).

In ancient Rome a person could not wear just any ring. Gold was allowed only for the holder of a military or civil rank. Silver was for a free person, and iron was for a slave.

True Roquefort cheese is aged in ancient caves in Roquefort, France.

A fortune-teller once told a young girl on the island of Martinique in the Caribbean that she would grow up to sit on a European throne. The girl later married Napolean Bonaparte and became the Empress Josephine of France.

In the Middle Ages animals were sometimes put on trial for crimes and executed.

The United States Treasury Department has a fund made up of money sent in by people for a variety of "conscience" reasons, both good and bad, including nonpayment of debts, cheating on their taxes, or even as a thank-you to the country.

Pompadoured wigs in France before the Revolution were sometimes as high as 3 feet.

Alaska has the longest coastline of any state: 34,000 miles.

The Verrazano-Narrows Bridge connecting Brooklyn to Staten Island, New York, is the longest suspension bridge in North America, with a length of 4,260 feet.

Sometimes the moon appears to be blue, because of sulfur particles in the atmosphere.

Evidence exists that surgical operations took place in prehistoric times. Saws used for amputations were hand-made of stone or bone.

Czar Peter I of Russia, who apparently could not grow a beard himself, ordered that all men must shave off their beards or pay a tax.

In 1938 a fish was caught in South African waters that scientists had believed to be extinct for about 50 million years. It was the coelacanth.

The first TV commercial was for the Bulova Watch Company in 1941.

Some birds require more than their weight in food each day.

During the American Revolution, when the British invaded Philadelphia, the Liberty Bell was secretly removed from Independence Hall and taken by wagon to Allentown, Pennsylvania, where it was hidden under the floorboards of a church. Had the bell remained in the state house, it would have been melted down for British ammunition, as were all the other bells of the city.

Sand was once used to dry hand-writing.

Cartoon was originally the first drawing for a mural, fresco, painting, stained glass, etc. Only recently has the term come to be used for humorous drawings or animated films.

Virginia Dare was the first white child of English parents born in the American Colonies, in 1587. She was named for the colony in which she was born.

For the movie *The Mummy,* actor Boris Karloff had to be baked into his makeup each day under heat lamps.

Krakatoa, a volcanic island between Sumatra and Java, exploded in 1883, killing 35,000 people.

Julius Erving's birthstone is the amethyst.

About 3,000 books are published each month in the United States.

CHECK OUT BOOKS HERE

About 70 percent of the earth's surface is water.

The earliest greeting card was a German "Happy New Year" greeting published in the 15th century.

The crust of the earth is between 10 and 30 miles thick.

There is no land at the North Pole. It is simply a mass of floating ice on the Arctic Ocean.

Potatoes contain more sugar than oranges.

The 200-inch lens of the world's largest telescope at Mount Palomar in California took 11 years to polish.

Some people believe that it is good luck to meet a flock of sheep.

If you speak to a duke, say "My Lord Duke." Address an emperor as "Sire" or "Your Imperial Majesty." An earl or a baron receives "My Lord" or a "Your Lordship," and a knight is "Sir."

In 1946 there were about 5,000 TV sets in the United States. By 1960 there were more than 50 million sets.

Benjamin Franklin had 16 brothers and sisters.

Women of the Nver tribe, who live in a swampy area of the Nile River, smoke pipes.

The central branch of the New York Public Library on Fifth Avenue has more than 80 miles of shelves, 5 million books, and 10 million nonbook materials. It also has 10,000 catalog drawers plus computer listings and services 2,000 people every day.

Atlantic City once had an "Elephant Hotel" built out of wood and used by the children of guests at a nearby hotel. The stairs to the upper floors were in the hind legs and the elephant's eyes were windows.

A cricket in your house is said to be a sign of good luck.

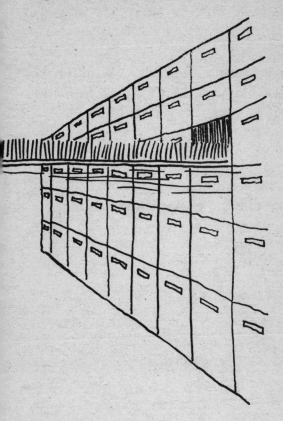

In Argentina, the "Man in the Moon" is upside down.

Elton John's real name is Reginald Kenneth Dwight.

Six-year-old Matthew Winkler of Lima, Ohio, was the first person in Ohio known to have survived rabies.

Chess grandmaster Bobby Fischer started playing chess at the age of 6.

Wall Street, famous today as the home of the stock market, was originally a wall that was built in 1653 to keep out Indians and wolves.

The world-famous vampire movie *Dracula* opened on St. Valentine's Day, 1931.

Scientists believe that the universe is anywhere from 13 to 18 billion years old.

In the elections of 1884 and 1888, a woman named Belva Lockwood ran for President of the United States.

Paul Revere had 16 children.

The largest desert in the world, the Sahara in north Africa, has some areas that are below sea level.

It is the law that a United States flag must never be used to cover a ceiling.

It is believed by some people that burning ears mean that someone is talking about you.

The oldest zoo in the United States is the Philadelphia Zoo, established in 1859. The first public zoo started in Paris in 1793.

The word *bookkeeper* has three successive sets of double letters in it.

Empress Marie Louise of France could fold her ears.

Colorado is called the Centennial State because it joined the Union in 1876, the hundredth birthday of the United States.

It takes several days for a mussel to move only a few inches.

Some experiments show that cows give more and better milk when they listen to music. The best results of all came with music by Mozart.

The poison of the passion flower causes convulsions of the face muscles. Therefore, a victim can look as if he is laughing himself to death.

It is said that if paper money is folded toward you more money will come. If it is folded away from you, it will soon be gone.

Koala "bears" are not bears at all— they are marsupials, mammals with pouches in which the young are raised.

Americans average about 42 hot dogs per person per year.

Japanese students studying for their college entrance exams must learn at least 1,850 Kanji (the ancient Chinese characters that form the structure of the Japanese language) in order to pass.

The United States once produced a ten dollar gold piece that was known as the *Eagle*.

Russia's Big Diomede Island off the coast of Siberia is only about 2½ miles away from the United States' Little Diomede Island, off the coast of Alaska, but they are a whole day apart because the international dateline comes down the Bering Strait between the two islands.

The John Pennekamp State Park in Florida is entirely underwater. The park is part of North America's only coral reef, and visitors swim through it wearing diving gear.

Some people say that it is bad luck to wash a blanket in a month that does not have an R in its name.

Revolutionary war hero John Paul Jones was really named John Paul, but added the name Jones to hide his identity. He had fled to the American Colonies to escape arrest after murdering a sailor.

Nails are an extension of the skin.

The movie screen at Philadelphia's Living History Center, built for the 1976 Bicentennial Exposition, is 70 feet by 93 feet, the world's largest. The projector that is used with it is more than 6 feet high.

The hummingbird is the only bird that can fly backward.

The only coins ever issued by Hawaii were the dime, quarter, and half-dollar issued by King Kalakaua I in 1883.

A coin collector is a *numismatist*. A stamp collector is a *philatelist*. Those who collect bugs are *entymologists*. Code experts are *cryptographers*.

A fathom is 6 feet long.

Raisins are called "sultanas" in England.

Mary, of "Mary Had a Little Lamb," was a real person, Mary Elizabeth Sawyer, who was born in 1806. The lamb followed her to school one day in the year 1815, at the Redstone Schoolhouse, outside of Boston.

Florence Nightingale, mother of modern nursing, willed her body to science, but her request was overruled and she was buried in an old family plot with her ancestors.

The northernmost and westernmost places on the North American continent are in the state of Alaska.

More hot dogs and soda are consumed by the people of Honolulu, Hawaii, than by people anywhere else in the United States.

The normal number of teeth for a human is 32.

If you write a letter to a king, you must address it to "The King's Most Excellent Majesty."

When the King and Queen of England visited President Franklin D. Roosevelt, he served them hot dogs.

Benjamin Franklin believed that women in the American Colonies had bad teeth because they ate hot soup and frozen apples.